Cries
against THE
Shepherds

Filtering Accusations
against Spiritual Leaders

aniel A. Brown, Ph.D.

Commended to The Word
ctW Equipping Leaders
for Ministry Impact.

Cries Against the Shepherds
© 2007 Daniel A. Brown, Ph.D.

Published by:
Commended to The Word
280 State Park Drive
Aptos, CA 95003
ctw.coastlands.org

Printed in the United States

Scripture quotations taken from New American Standard Bible® Copyright The Lockman Foundation 1960, 1962, 1963, 1968, 1971, 1972, 1973, 1975, 1977, 1995.

ISBN 978-0-9779173-2-7

Cries Against the Shepherds

How do we filter accusations against spiritual leaders
to ensure that selfish, controlling shepherds are brought
to repentance without also bringing selfless shepherds
to impotence?

---

*... they have opened the wicked and deceitful mouth against me;
they have spoken against me with a lying tongue. They have also
surrounded me with words of hatred, and fought against me without
cause. In return for my love they act as my accusers...*

– King David circa 1000 B.C.

S piritual abuse in the church isn't a recent phenomenon.
Shepherds who mishandle their spiritual role by mistreating people
the Lord has entrusted to their care have been around since before
the times of Jeremiah and Ezekiel when God rebuked spiritual leaders for
leading His sheep astray (see Jeremiah 23 and Ezekiel 34).

Numerous spiritual authorities have violated God's people for their own
gain—from Lucifer and the angels to the evil-doing kings of Israel and
Judah; from King Saul to Corinthian pseudo-apostles; from *"Diotrephes,
who loves to be first"* (3 John 9) to *"false teachers who secretly introduce
destructive heresies"* in the first century (2 Peter 2:1). Our modern-day
newspapers catalog the same sort of violation among twenty-first century
congregations.

No one can deny the continued existence of sinfully driven, selfishly motivated spiritual leaders. Despite the best efforts of denominations to weed out clergy who are pastoring for unrighteous motives, insecure and insincere leaders still find their way into the ranks of spiritual leadership. That does not even begin to account for the many leaders whose best intentions for ministry fall short either because of their inexperience or their mistaken choices. Clergy can and do take advantage of their congregations in order to fulfill their own selfish needs.

Because of God's choice to arrange the world in such a way that leaders—such as parents, school teachers, counselors—have an extraordinary impact on people's lives, unprincipled leaders do tremendous damage to the psyche of the people under them. Since church leaders add a spiritual dimension to the equation, they can do double damage. People tend to be more open to spiritual authorities than to most other types of leaders.

Consequently, wrongly motivated church leaders wreak greater havoc in lives than do the sins of a non-leader. Because they are trusted with access to vulnerable places in others' lives, leaders' careless words, frustrations and petty indignations affect people more strongly than do those same carnal manifestations coming from peers.

Abuse by Leaders

Abuse is the exploitation of people for the purpose of providing a person in authority with something (unrighteous) he or she wants. Through error or deceitfulness, abusive shepherds cause the "little ones to stumble." They mislead people with false words or with actions that are out of character with the heart of Father God. Abuse by spiritual leaders comes in many forms:

1. **False Teaching** and consistent misinterpretations of Scripture distort the essence and truth of the Gospel (Galatians 1:6–10 and 2 John 7–11).

2. **Control and Manipulation** force people to deny their personal freedom and responsibility in God in order to obey and please the leader (1 Thessalonians 2:3-6 and 2 Corinthians 5:9-15).

3. **Inappropriate Relationships** and connections with vulnerable church-members intentionally "set up" by the leader cause members to fall (2 Timothy 3:2-9 and 2 Peter 2:13-19).

4. **Pseudo-Authority** emphasizes the importance of followers' *submission*, more than leaders' *servanthood* (Mark 10:42-45 and Colossians 1:24-29).

It is staggering to consider how dreadfully people have been hurt by unrighteous spiritual leaders. With every instance of violated trust, when people's vulnerability is exploited by those to whom they have disclosed the tender places of their life, authority figures are viewed with more and more suspicion.

Allegations of dishonesty or physical abuse by members of the clergy are rare. That is because truly criminal and dangerous spiritual leaders are, likewise, few in number. God's people must be warned against the danger of manipulative, controlling leaders who masquerade as spiritual guides. But those people must also be alerted to the dangerous temptation of jumping to conclusions that condemn leaders for leading. Manipulative people can exploit legitimate concerns about spiritual abuse for their own purposes.

Wolf Cries

Bad church leaders not only introduce personal trauma and disillusionment that can take years to erase, but those false shepherds also cause reproach and distrust to fall upon godly, caring spiritual authorities. That misgiving can easily create a danger of its own—the danger of spiritual abuse from the bottom up. In our zeal to protect the sheep, we can respond too quickly to the cry of "wolf" when someone in a church claims to have been spiritually abused by a present or former leader.

False accusations against godly, strong leaders and gross misinterpretations of normal conflicts within a church threaten the church worldwide. When the boy falsely cried "wolf," the people ended up not responding when the cry of alarm was genuine. When sheep erroneously point at a shepherd and cry "wolf," the implications are far grimmer than diminished wariness toward future attacks.

The shepherd's entire future can be hung in the *false* balance.

That's why the Bible tells us not to accept an accusation against an elder except in the case where more than one person can verify it (1 Timothy

5:19). That does not mean two or three people who have heard the same story—and then pass it along as truth (that's called gossip). Paul recommends suspending judgment *until* an accusation against a leader is corroborated by more than one witness to a specific violation/sin. He isn't talking about being accused of generalized wrong-doing or about disputes when followers grow disillusioned with a leader.

Everyone is against spiritual abuse. No one wants to unintentionally participate in a cover-up of abuse in church. Spiritual abuse clearly deserves condemnation, but the heaviness of the crime sometimes adds its weightiness to the scales of justice—tipping them toward presumed guilt. The speed with which everyone wants to remove a guilty abuser from ministry can unintentionally become the speed with which anyone *accused* of that activity is preemptively condemned.

Lingering Suspicion

Abuse is a *buzz word*. No specific proof is required for a charge that vague. Even if the generic accusation eventually gets refuted by an accused pastor, the lingering clouds of suspicion that hang around his or her ministry are extremely difficult to dispel. If the church leader tries to counter the charges with specific facts, it can be seen as defensiveness—a tacit admission of guilt.

Claims of spiritual abuse feed off one another, and very soon there is little, if any, interest in specifics or accounts of actual error. There were many witnesses who brought accusation against Jesus, but their complaints were vague generalities or inconsistent accounts (Mark 14:55-59 and John 18:29-30). Even when no actual wrong has been found (John 19:6), the lynch-cry of a crowd against the accused quickly echoes what Pilate heard: "Crucify!"

The genuine sufferers of abuse—not to mention the pastors who are falsely accused of being abusers—deserve a careful and thoughtful examination of specific claims against church leaders. We do no one any good by rushing out with haste and excessive zeal in particular cases just because we want to address a generalized problem in the church. People are naturally inclined to *pick up* others' offenses, and become indignant at how others were treated.

> *Unfounded and unsubstantiated allegations devastate their target.*

Whatever the motive behind false or ill-informed accusations, cries that an off-base church leader has been abusive meet with sympathetic approval and concern. When individuals express their pain, it's very tempting to rush to their emotional defense—forgetting that we're only hearing one side of the story.

The Accuser

Gossip and slander have been around since Adam and Eve listened to the first devilish charges leveled against God. Unfounded and unsubstantiated allegations devastate their target. That is why they are so often employed by the "Father of Lies." Slanderous claims produce crippling fear in the accused one's heart, and they create tremendous self-doubt in sincere leaders: *Am I crazy? Did I really do that? How could this be happening? Why would people believe this? Have I failed so miserably?*

The devil is aptly named *"the Accuser of our brethren"* (Revelation 12:10).

The Bible says a great deal about slander and accusation, and how often they are used by our Adversary to cripple the Church. The Enemy of the Church knows the principle of striking down the shepherd and scattering the sheep.

We celebrate Moses as an excellent role-model, yet Moses drew disproportionate amounts of criticism and opposition. Though the Bible calls him the most humble of men, he faced the strongest accusations from elders and fellow leaders who decided that he thought too highly of himself. Throughout the exodus, Moses'

> *Crippling accusations will come against spiritual leaders who dare "to seek the welfare of the sons of Israel".* (Neh. 2:10)

followers leveled charge after charge against him because of their "greedy desires" (Numbers 11:4) and their foolish compulsion to return to a familiar place of bondage (Numbers 14:1-4).

Miriam and Aaron, two prophetic and priestly leaders who should have known better, "spoke against" Moses because they did not approve of his choice to marry Zipporah (Numbers 12:1-2). Not long afterwards, several well-known and highly respected leaders rose up in complaint against Moses because they thought he had assumed a leadership position above everyone else (Numbers 16:1-3). The accusations were not spawned by anything Moses had done, but by what the accusers had concluded about him.

In addition, Joseph's brothers came to conclusions about his motives and self-image, and had it not been for one brother's intervention, they would have murdered him. Absalom usurped David's rule by claiming that David was insensitive to people's legitimate needs. The list of leaders in the Bible who underwent accusation and opposition by those they served is quite long. That is no accident of history!

As they have from the earliest days of ministry, crippling accusations will come against spiritual leaders who dare "to seek the welfare of the sons of Israel" (Nehemiah 2:10). Just as Sanballat invented private and public indictments to intimidate Nehemiah, hoping to back him away from his ministry (Nehemiah 4:2-14), so our Enemy still plots against spiritual leaders today.

Deadly Shafts

Words can hurt a reputation. Juicy bits of accusing gossip float around our churches, tempting us to partake. Whispered complaints are "like dainty morsels" that people swallow only too eagerly (Proverbs 26:22); they are like an ambushing barrage of arrows so deadly sharp that they pierce almost any shield (Proverbs 25:18). There is no defense against them. Many, many pastors have been knocked out of ministry by such barbed shafts that were aimed by the Enemy but loosed by the lips of naïve believers.

Innuendo and whispers can call into question years and years of a pastor's faithful ministry by fooling people into spreading the slander (Proverbs 10:18). We pass along tidbits, hearsay, and unsubstantiated conclusions about others, taking our place in the bucket-brigade of gossip, slander and accusation, and throwing gasoline on fires of misinformation. People's lives get ruined. Jesus said that slander (like murder, envy and pride) is spawned from within us, out of our own heart, and it defiles us (Mark

7:21-23). Jesus admonished us to concentrate on the beam in our own eye and not to judge…lest we be judged.

When we disagree with someone—especially a leader—we're more eager than we'd like to admit to find something that person said or did that confirms our disregard. Oh, how we love to be able to say to ourselves, "I knew it! I've had a funny feeling about her all along." Like the Pharisees of old, we're on the lookout for others doing something unlawful, so we can deliver our pronouncement on it (and them). It all feels so righteous, so true; after all, we're simply protecting others from being misled or abused by leaders who might otherwise go undetected.

Motives for Slander

Just because a leader is accused of something, it does not mean the accusations are true. The saying "*Where there is smoke, there must be fire*" isn't necessarily biblical. Accusations aren't like smoke: smoke always comes from some type of combustion. Accusations, on the other hand, can come from many different sources and with many different motives.

"Tickle my ears…"

For instance, some people want their ears tickled (2 Timothy 4:3), and when a leader says things with which they do not agree or that differ from their perspective, they find many ways not to listen—one of the most effective being to vilify the leader. Many "wolf" cries are intentional acts of revenge against leaders who tried to dismantle individuals' peculiar ministry perspectives and their mental strongholds (2 Corinthians 10:3-6).

Final Frames
My *"Takes"* on
Ministry for a Lifetime

"These biblical perspectives formed the ballast stones of my entire pastoral ministry. They kept me focused in the face of confusion or despair, and they gave me courage when dwarfed by giants. They were the measures by which I countered every lie and counted every gain.

I only wish an older mentor had shared such with me far, far earlier in my ministry..."

Daniel A. Brown, Ph.D.

Other teachings from Daniel A. Brown, Ph.D.

Ministry Gift Mixes - *Audio*
Discover the unique ways God has designed people! Identifying ministry gift mixes within your church will...
- Foster better communication
- Reveal how your strengths and weaknesses work together
- Explain why we differ in our responses to the same situations

Deliverance - *Audio*
Demonic influence can be a controversial and often misunderstood topic. Clarity comes with understanding...
- What demons are, and how they influence people
- The biblical foundations for deliverance ministry
- How to pray for people to be freed from the power of evil

Timely and True Spirituals - *Audio*
True spirituality doesn't always look very religious or powerful. Entering the supernatural realm simply means...
- Obeying the smallest instruction from the Lord
- Judging prophetic words, dreams, pictures and promptings
- Understanding the purpose of and power behind our spiritual language

Message to the Exiled - *Audio*
Poor choices or others' sinful actions can leave us in a discouraging place we can't change. That's exile. Discover...
- Why a good God allows tragedy
- How to live with a less-than-perfect past
- What to do if you're stuck in a destructive cycle

Enjoying Your Journey with God - *Book*
Come face-to-face with a God who delights in you! This practical, non-religious guide offers the foundations for Christian faith.
- Understand the amazing love and kindness of God
- Learn how to resist daily temptations
- Great for small group studies or discussion

Let me give you an example.

Through the years, some people have sought validation from me, but on the wrong basis. They insisted on proving their (spiritual) worth by *teaching* me on every occasion they could find because, in their mindset, "biblical knowledge" was the primary measure of spirituality. They subconsciously believed that the more they could prove how much they knew, the more they would be approved in my eyes. Forgetting Paul's reminder that knowledge "puffs [us] up," but love builds others up (1 Corinthians 8:1), some long-term Christians become confused about the primacy of love.

Every week for months, a man approached me immediately after service to share his understandings about additional points and information that should have been taught from the sermon text. Even when I invited new converts to come meet me at the conclusion of the service, he managed to arrive first and forced me to attend to his "thoughts" before I could greet them. Eventually, his rigidity and blindness stole away my enthusiasm and hope for his ministry.

"Why not take all you know and start a Bible study?" I finally inquired. Because he had never been able to attract people into the grim sphere of his stern religiousness, he took my question as rejection. Once I ceased being his captive audience, he declared me a false shepherd.

Hidden Agenda

When someone talks to us about another person, what we're hearing might easily be prejudiced—intentionally or unintentionally—by a hidden agenda that probably won't be spoken aloud. However, that agenda will color the "facts" in the story. Talebearers are not trustworthy witnesses (Proverbs 11:13). Jealousy, bitterness, fear-of-failure, covetousness—all these and many more evils of the heart can motivate people to reveal compromising information about others, instead of covering them in love (1 Peter 4:8).

This is especially true when people make negative comments and speak unkindly about someone's pastor. It's quite rattling to have our confidence in a spiritual leader challenged because we're being told that we cannot believe our eyes and ears. If we missed seeing all the bad things that were going on under our noses, we start feeling insecure. According to the Word of God, hidden "hatred" stirs up strife among believers, claiming its only motive is to open people's eyes to what's going on (Proverbs 10:12). But what is the motive really?

I remember asking one person why he kept attending our Saturday services after he had informed me that I was a false leader who squelched prophetic words in our congregation. Some weeks earlier, he had delivered one of those ultimatum-type prophecies that was both unclear and generally condemning. Because I loved him and his teen-age boys, and because I knew he was new at these sorts of things, I agreed to share the word with our pastoral staff to get their "judgment" of it. They rejected its validity, and I had met again with the man to woo him to a place of reason, allowing for a simple learner's mistake (as opposed to a false prophecy). He denounced me on the spot, and announced my untrustworthiness to many people.

Seeing him continue to attend our services aroused my curiosity; his reply to my inquiry was simple, "I am here to prevent what you did to me from happening to others!" And, according to three people who had conversed with him between services, to invite people from our church to attend his new church—"where the pastor can be trusted."

Likewise, a woman who was passed over for a ministry position "everyone knew should have been hers" stopped going to our church but wanted to alert friends from the church to my spiritual corruption. Using herself as a case in point, she revealed how manipulative I was, getting what I wanted with false promises. Her complaint against me was masked as a sincere warning to others: "Don't get too close or let yourself be used by *that* pastor. You should see what he did to me and my family!"

What really happened in the counseling session when I carefully explained why I could not promote her in more ministry, would never be told. I made no rebuttal to her charges because I would not call attention to what disqualified her from assuming more responsibility in the church: the legalistic and judgmental manner with which she handled people. There was no way to righteously deflect the lies coming from her lips (Proverbs 10:18).

Self-Justification

One of the primary agendas hidden beneath accusations against spiritual leaders is simple self-justification. Evil reports against a cell group leader or a ministry director are often attempts to harm the reputation of someone who brought instruction or correction to the accuser. People absolve themselves of responsibility to heed unwanted counsel if they can discredit the advisor. That's what Solomon meant when he said:

He who corrects a scoffer gets dishonor for himself, and he who reproves a wicked man gets insults for himself. Do not reprove a scoffer, or he will hate you...

Proverbs 9:7-8

If people can be convinced in their own minds that lots of things are wrong with their spiritual leader, it makes rejecting his or her counsel much easier.

Quite early in the life of our church, we had an incident of a lonely single mom falling too quickly—and too far—for a guy. After a couple of weeks, the woman realized her mistake, and chose to reestablish appropriate boundaries. That frustrated the man, and it quickly became evident that he was an angry, disturbed man whose Christian façade was thin—and thinning even further.

Trying to play the role of unsuspecting innocent who simply had befriended the kids and been sucked into the woman's *neediness*, he refused any counsel I offered him about getting his life back on track. He wanted to blame the woman for seducing him, and when he subsequently became a peeping Tom, frightening her and her kids by stalking them, I told him, after several counseling sessions, he was unwelcome in the church unless he stopped his odd behavior.

His peculiar fixation on the woman—and the peace it stole away from her and her young children—was not recounted when he claimed how unloving I had been to him, and how I cut him out of the church. As a young and somewhat inexperienced pastor, I was shocked at how rapidly the issue became about me, instead of him. Though I cannot say for certain, I seriously doubt that he spent much time confessing his faults while condemning mine in conversation with people.

Though he was very reluctant to get counsel, he was eager to offer it: he advised others not to go to our church any longer because of the way I treated him. It was unchristian, unloving and prejudiced in favor of the woman "who spread all sorts of lies" about him. He wanted me to pay for what I did, and in order for my wrongs to replace his as the topic of discussion, he had to portray me as guilty of gross violations: I never listened to him; I condemned him; I was a control-freak trying to act like everyone's father; I asked women about their sexual lives; I was abusive and egotistical…

The man was after me! My hope during those dark days was that people read their Bible and remembered scriptures like,

> *The thoughts of the righteous are just, but the counsels of the wicked are deceitful. The words of the wicked lie in wait for blood…*

> *Proverbs 12:5-6*

Over-the-Shoulder Shot

Christians sometimes have serious disputes with other Christians. It even happens with close friends—more often than we might think. Like Barnabus and Paul, people who minister together can come to disagree so sharply about spiritual issues or ministry philosophy that they separate from one another (Acts 15:39). There is no indication whatsoever from the Scriptures about who was right in that first century conflict. Because of his prominence in the book of Acts, we might be tempted to side with

Paul against Barnabus—until we recall that John Mark, the young man Paul had given up on, became one of the Gospel writers.

Here's the point: Sometimes, two individuals see matters so differently and so passionately that they cannot walk together (Amos 3:3). This does not mean that they cannot love and celebrate one another, but it does mean that they will go different directions. Christian unity is not uniformity; rather, it is a determination to look beyond our differences and to forgive those who offend us.

If one of the disagreeing people is the leader of the other, it is especially difficult. The leader feels betrayed; the former follower feels abused. Most likely, the member of the church, rather than the pastor, ends up leaving the church. The collateral damage of severed

> *Sometimes, two individuals see matters so differently and so passionately that they cannot walk together (Amos 3:3).*

connection with the pastor usually leads to a subsequent loss of vital connection with other members of the church left behind. It is painful, and it seems very unfair, to lose the ongoing depth of relationship formerly enjoyed with others in the church. That pain seeks an outlet.

Sometimes hurting people deal with their pain by blaming a "bad guy," or by wanting to convince friends in the former church how wrong (abusive) their leader has been. How sad it is for "offended" people to try drawing others into their camp of opposition against another child of God, but how common it has been since the earliest days of the Church:

I have been informed concerning you... that there are quarrels among you. Now I mean this, that each one of you is saying, 'I am of Paul,' and 'I of Apollos,' and 'I of Cephas,' and 'I of Christ.' Has Christ been divided? Paul was not crucified for you, was he? Or were you baptized in the name of Paul?

1 Corinthians 1:11-13

Far more biblical would be a simple willingness to part company and go separate ways, believing the best of one another and agreeing to disagree.

Once someone casts a disagreement as a matter of conscience, and turns the way leaders have done things into issues of right vs. wrong, that person becomes a crusader. Crusaders want to battle, not reconcile, and they enlist fellow crusaders in righteous indignation by recounting wrongs they and others have suffered.

How we leave a church or a season that has ended is very, very telling about our character. I know how I want the Lord to speak of my past: I rely on His grace to cover my sins and forget my iniquities, so I believe my calling is to treat past leaders' mistakes the same way. I have not always been successful because my desire to be right has clouded my judgment and urged me, also, to "hint" at leaders' problems. God has had to *help* me more than once!

How we leave a church or a season that has ended is very, very telling about our character.

Like the time at our denominational convention years and years ago when the Lord told me to confess my smallness, my conceit, my attitude—

and my unkind words—to our president. Yikes! Confession is terribly humbling...but profoundly strengthening against future temptations.

When people want to accuse another person, I have learned to sift their stories with a simple filter: is the accuser relating specific episodes, comments and sins that strike them as out of character for the accused one to be doing/saying, or is the accuser subtly asking me to condemn the whole person?

Many church members interpret a pastor's behavior and conversation in light of their disappointments with their parents or spouse.

Authority Figures

Relationship with spiritual leaders is complicated even further because, as "authority figures," pastors often end up representing every unfulfilled or broken relationship parishioners have had with important people in their past. Many church members interpret a pastor's behavior and conversation in light of their disappointments with their parents or spouse.

Grown men whose fathers failed to speak kind words can become so attached to a spiritual leader's favor that it is unhealthy. A woman with an abusive father and/or mother who coldly rejects her repeatedly may invest too much of herself in relationship with her pastor—and then be disproportionately pained when that connection ceases to meet her expectations. That pain, too, seeks an expression.

At one point in my years at The Coastlands, I became aware of idolatry— staff members and followers who looked too intently to me for answers and direction. Their *unfathered* childhood was a setup for making my part in their lives, and theirs in mine, fraught with the possibility of spiritual calamity. Knowing that they would dismiss my concerns (or blame me for them), I relinquished my role as a counseling pastor to them. I simply stopped offering advice. That change disillusioned them, and it wasn't long before they had more internal motivation to disdain me than to revere me.

Though it is awkward and ungainly to cast oneself down, idols cannot be allowed to keep their place. Far better to be the object of others' indignation than of their (unintended) idolatry. Being a pastor is also sometimes like being wealthy—people want your friendship...but not always because of you! Spiritual leaders must be somewhat vigilant to identify church members who hope to gain from the connection.

Years ago I elected to distance myself from individuals whom I felt were using their association with me to intimidate others—and to curry special favor. Several times I observed (and later challenged) the way they monopolized conversations and used my name like a credit card to push their agenda. The pain I went through was considerable when those "close" friends vehemently turned on me and named me the world's worst defrauder. It was easy for them to cast the drama as a story of abandonment, indicting me with a rhetorical question: "What kind of a pastor uses people until they need him, then abandons them?"

Revenge

On more than one occasion, former church members and past ministry associates did their best to convince unsuspecting members of my congregation that, despite the healing and blessing they experienced during my leadership, I was actually an evil man who secretly destroyed people's lives. Of course, such charges would strike at the heart of every godly leader. We who pastor with any integrity at all, know what phonies we are! Every time we preach or counsel or lead, we are afraid that we will ruin people by saying or doing the wrong thing!

That is why true spiritual leaders are so rocked by accusation—even the outlandish ones! Most pastors I know can tell stories of multiple accusers, and we have all echoed David's prayer, seeking refuge from the "well-conceived plot" of evildoers who aimed "bitter speech" of invented injustices at us (Psalm 64:1-4).

A disgruntled couple, who came to us from a dissimilar church tradition, had a radically different view than I did on a few key points of ministry. The disagreement was not about any essential doctrine. They tended to be literalists (of the few verses they remembered) who missed the context of verses on women, divorce, submission, etc. But I was happy to pastor and teach them. From every indication, they were happy, too, for several years—until their daughter failed to be accepted into our internship training program. I could not appropriately disclose to them the reasons why. I urged the girl to acknowledge certain issues to her parents, but she was in her early 20's and had to be free, in my opinion, to make her own decisions about what she would tell her parents.

Not long after, the couple and their daughter moved to another state, ostensibly for financial reasons, and I was shaken when, a couple of years later, they *and* their daughter wrote letters accusing me of teaching false doctrine (no specifics were included in the letter to my supervisor). *"How ridiculous,"* said my mind; *"What if it's true and you just don't realize it?"* asked my heart...

I was so rattled by the accusation because I had no context for it. My theology went something like this: speak the truth in love and everyone will be grateful for the rescue. Not a very adequate theology to prepare a young minister for the realities of leading a church. And not even a very biblical theology in light of Paul's struggles with people who would not "endure sound doctrine," but turned away their ears (see 2 Timothy 2-4).

From Jesus to David, spiritual leaders in the Bible had to deal with betrayal and revenge—especially by formerly close associates:

Even my close friend in whom I trusted, who ate my bread, has lifted up his heel against me.

Psalm 41:9

All my trusted friends, watching for my fall, say: Perhaps he will be deceived, so that we may prevail against him and take our revenge on him.

Jeremiah 20:10

Jesus answered them, 'Did I Myself not choose you, the twelve, and yet one of you is a devil?'

John 6:70

Jesus' words are strong: "One of you is a *devil!*" It might surprise many Christians to learn that the word translated *devil* [*diabolos*] isn't referring to Judas being a demon, but is more accurately translated *false accuser, slanderer*! The word's essence—and one of the key components of demonic assault in our lives—is to bring charges against someone with hostile intent. Judas listened to the devil's accusations against Jesus, and after "Satan entered into

Judas" (Luke 22:3), those internal whispers eventually created a reasonable justification for betrayal.

Controlling Leader?

The *easiest-to-make* indictment against a spiritual leader is that he or she is *controlling*. It is a word that strikes healthy dread in every godly leader. Jonestown, Waco and other scenes of lost life loom at the end of the road taken by controlling leaders. Before it is too late, we want to stop cult-like leaders. The urgency to prevent future disasters makes the Body of Christ susceptible to people within a church who know how to work the theme to gain revenge against a leader who told them a truth they didn't want to hear.

The point is not that leaders are always right, and people in church should just submit to whatever their leaders do or say. That kind of blind submission and fatalism goes against the spirit of the New Testament. Any leader who *demands* submission is not a leader we should follow.

> *The easiest-to-make indictment against a spiritual leader is that he or she is controlling.*

There is a huge difference, however, between imposing one's own will and pointing out God's will. For instance, I was called controlling when I refused to surrender our church service into the hands of a self-styled prophet. He wanted to hijack the church and steer it on an angry course, spewing judgment against everyone except himself and any who agreed with him. A huge part of my ministry philosophy always centered on *proof in the pudding*: true leaders gather their own followers by living out and speaking God's words; they do not insist upon followers being handed to them by another leader.

Because I contended for the development of spiritual giftedness in my own congregation, as opposed to training them to be a good audience

> *Any leader who demands*
> *submission is not a leader*
> *we should follow.*

for ministers more expert than can generally be produced at a typical local church, I'm sure we missed out on some of the "words" and revelations that such

outside ministers would have brought to us. That was ok with me. I gladly accepted the trade-off: less awareness among my congregation of themes and messages popular on the national church circuit, and more awareness of our responsibility to minister to one another.

But I was called controlling.

There is no suitable defense against the charge. Sheep can be easily swayed away from their congregations by those who tell partial or slanted versions of their stories. Once charged, evidence seems to surface on its own from the most unexpected sources, like it did from a man who had left our church after several months of unsuccessful ministry and counseling. His marriage was in trouble, he felt almost no personal connection with the Lord in his heart, and he had a hard time getting along with people—since he was always right.

He was tormented by thousands of *what if* fears and wrong conclusions about what God needed to do to fix his problems. Instead of being still and allowing God to be God, this man tried to solve his own predicaments by giving God action ultimatums. He gave advice to God with his eyes closed, and called it prayer. He was miserable…and usually stressed or defeated. I offered him sound biblical advice that somehow, in the two years since he had left our church, got reinterpreted as ungodly *manipulation*.

My heartfelt counsel to him had been, *"Quit thinking so much!"* When quoted out of context and with a different tone of voice than I had used when speaking those words in love, they were made to sound like the mantra of a controlling leader telling his followers not to think for themselves, but to follow his mandates instead.

Call to Repentance

As ministers, our assignment is to represent God and to serve people. We cannot truly serve people by misrepresenting God's Word or His ways. And His ways *always* call for people to repent, to reconsider their ways. Most discipling and counseling calls for people to repent of their own way of thinking or behaving.

But not everyone wants to change. Many people want to be confirmed in their thinking or behaving. They want counseling, but only if that counseling will leave their assumptions and conclusions intact. When they encounter ministers who challenge those assumptions and conclusions, these people look for a way to discredit those ministers in order to keep from having to change themselves.

"The pastor wasn't nice to me" is a socially acceptable way of saying, "He was wrong to challenge me and tell me to reconsider my conclusions." The victim of an abusive spiritual leader elicits tremendous sympathy in our Christian sub-culture; the person who refuses to take sound, biblical counsel does not. When individuals complain they have been abused by a controlling pastor, it sounds much more legitimate than admitting they chose not to take the biblical advice their pastor offered to them.

Limited Disclosure

Most of the time when leaders are accused, only half of the story gets told— by those whose antagonism toward that leader "stirs up strife" (Proverbs 10:12). To keep from uncovering the woundedness or corruption in people, church leaders must pay a huge personal cost: they know that "love covers a multitude of sins" (1 Peter 4:8), and when falsely accused, they do not want to uncover others' sin to defend themselves. It is an agonizing bind for godly leaders.

> *To keep from uncovering the woundedness or corruption in people, church leaders must pay a huge personal cost and when falsely accused, they do not want to uncover others' sin to defend themselves.*

Except for a few members of our pastoral team, my congregation knew nothing about a particular woman's manic-depressive condition that manifested in mental swings between suicidal thoughts and bridal fantasies (like dressing up night after night, expecting me to pick her up and carry her away to a new life and ministry together). In close counsel with her husband, I took measures to keep a healthy distance from her and to keep from encouraging her delusions. We agreed that her son would not end up on the soccer team I coached next season, and they would seek a new church home.

Was that abusive control or mercy? Between her tragic emotional flip-flops, she seemed quite normal, so her slanderous words against my integrity roused sympathy (toward her) and suspicion (toward me). I couldn't legitimately speak ill of her to defend myself, so I bore the brunt of her vengeful gossip. In such instances, I felt my course must be to keep others covered…and to trust that God would cover me.

It is unethical (and usually illegal) for pastors to reveal what has been said in the privacy of the "confessional"; it's the spiritual counterpart to client/attorney privilege. No one can respect or trust leaders who uncover others by violating that supposed sanctity. I know pastors who have disclosed sensitive information I shared with them in counseling/confession. Nothing has strained my relationship with those pastors more than that violation.

But without revealing very private and sensitive information about people, pastors are often left without a way to explain why something was done or said. For example, a church leader cannot ethically disclose the abuses of a husband that make it unconscionable to urge his wife to return to the husband's control—for a third time. And yet, exclaiming that the Bible taught that his wife "had to submit" to him, such a husband was a co-conspirator in one of the fiercest seasons of accusation against me in the 22 years I pastored.

Simple Questions

Church leaders can be as boorish, as insensitive and as selfish as any other human. No one can deny that simple reality. But we ought to remember that false accusations against spiritual leaders have been a favorite disruptive ploy of the devil throughout the ages. Accusers prefer the safety of shadows to exploit the issue of spiritual abuse for their own ends. It can be an avenue of perfect revenge to "get back" at a leader who didn't do what a church member wanted done.

When the pastor is second-guessed by individuals who have a vested interest in finding fault, the known "facts" can easily be distorted to sketch an ugly portrait of the leader. Accusers' motives are not always upfront, so, let us pause a moment in the headlong rush to condemn an accused shepherd by asking ourselves some simple questions:

- What does this bearer-of-tales want me to do with what he is sharing?

- Has the accuser sought to address his grievance with the one who hurt him, in order to give the supposed offender an opportunity to shed light on misunderstandings and/or to offer an apology?

- Who else has been told? Do any of those (who have been told) have a role of leadership or oversight in the life of the offender?

- What is the ultimate goal—does the tale bearer want help in getting past the pain, or does he want allies in a campaign against the accused?

- What is the accuser's response if we offer to go to the offender, with a *specific* list of complaints and allegations, to seek clarification and reconciliation?

Generally speaking, the more people an accuser tells about what was done to him, the more likely his ultimate intention is revenge, not reconciliation or recovery. Payback is a huge motivator. That's why the Bible is so full of cautions against taking our own revenge; we're supposed to leave room for God to do His work and requite to people (including leaders) the justice due them (Romans 12:19).

Bona Fide Mistakes

Counsel is not objective; neither is the shaping process of discipleship. When we mentor people by alerting them to God's ways (which are not like theirs) and by warning them about points of sin or disobedience in their lives, we are engaged in the primary mandate of our own life. Making disciples is taking risks. It cannot be done by formula or by academic instruction alone.

That means we will, at times, emphasize the wrong things or even miss what God is really saying. Spiritually, we can misdiagnose the problem: we might try to comfort people's hurt instead of confronting their bitterness (or vice versa); we may think we are dealing with pride when it is really fear; what seems like a *sinful* choice to purchase pornography might actually be indications of *demonic* bondage to lust. Discernment is always a judgment call.

That sobering reality ought to strike a healthy fear in those of us who attempt to minister to people. The possibility that we can read situations or people incorrectly ought to drive us to radical accountability and personal repentance. Along with a determined prayer life and avid Bible reading, we who minister to others must welcome constant conviction ourselves.

As a senior pastor, I did dumb things in private, *and* I did dumb things in public. I was and am a sinner! My clay feet loomed like boulders beneath me, and I unintentionally trampled many sensitive situations with them. My timing has been off; I've used poor word-choices; I've hurt feelings by how I arranged seating for a staff luncheon, and how I didn't give an adequate send-off to departing staff; I've forgotten to inform people of changes before they discovered those changes in the bulletin. I challenged people at the wrong times and in the wrong ways; I was, at times, too

Making disciples is taking risks.

strong, too weak, too opinionated, too vacillating, too eager and too reluctant. I got too close to some people, and not close enough to others…

Whole-heartedly do I admit to these and many more mistakes. Gladly would I seek forgiveness from anyone I hurt in the dozens upon dozens of instances when my carnal nature spun me down a wrong path and caused me to crash into beloved believers who called me pastor.

But that admission and that willingness to say "I'm sorry" isn't enough when a leader faces the fury of abuse from the bottom up in church; when accusers have a crusade agenda and are interested in much, much more than restored relationship with a pastor; when they want the pastor ruined…

Scattered Words

I heard the story of a pastor in the Midwest who endured several years of accusation by a couple who later admitted they were just angry and disappointed with the pastor for not doing what they expected him to do. Their sense that he owed them more partnership in ministry than he eventually gave them caused them to malign his entire ministry. Having been slighted, they sought to diminish his standing in the eyes of others.

They had related their stories of abusive practices to anyone who would listen—often initiating conversations to get back in touch with former friends from the church "out of concern" that they, too, may have been unfairly treated. A subtle innuendo here, a slight criticism there, and the couple had opportunity to spread a clever wedge of slander to separate people from their former pastor (Proverbs 16:28). They were then able to say, "We've talked to lots of people who have been hurt like we were."

After confessing their sin of slander to their former pastor, and expressing their heartfelt desire to take back all they had said, they asked for forgiveness—which the pastor readily gave.

"But," he asked, "How difficult would it be to pick up all the pieces of this newspaper if you cut it into small 1-inch squares and scattered it like confetti from the top of the water-tower downtown on a windy day?"

"Impossible," they replied.

"Exactly. And the winds of gossip have taken your words of slander and condemnation where they cannot be called back. People will come across your words for years to come."

That is the lasting legacy of false accusation.

Other teachings from Daniel A. Brown Ph.D.

Jezebel–A Controlling Spirit that Splits Churches
Deceptive and slippery, the spirit of Jezebel is difficult to pin down, leaving us feeling uneasy, depressed and hopeless. Discover how Jezebel:
- Silences leaders
- Derails congregations
- *Can be overcome!*

Strategic Planning for the Local Church
Fully participating in God's plan means we can strategically arrange the elements of our church. Unify your congregation by:
- Understanding your mission
- Finding your church's focus
- Recognizing your existing and your ideal church

The Problem with…The Problem with Women in Ministry Leadership
Why are so many sincere believers convinced that only men should be spiritual leaders? Explore the truth about women:
- Covering their heads in church
- Speaking during worship services
- Teaching or having authority over a man

The Power Behind Giving & Tithing
Prosperity isn't about what you keep; it's about what you give away. Learn about:
- How to "plant" your money and watch it grow
- God's spiritual retirement plan
- The difference between luck and blessing

Church with Attitude
Church becomes dynamic and meaningful in the 21st century when we discover:
- The fast track to spiritual growth—individually and corporately
- How to foster accessibility and accountability
- How to mobilize servant-hearted leaders

If you would like to receive a free download of *How to Mobilize Your Church*, please enter the coupon code, SHEPHERD, during your next order. Offer expires 12/31/07

Visit our website for more...
ctw.coastlands.org